Standing In God's Promises

Precious Cody

Self-Published: Precious Cody

Limits of Liability- Disclaimer
The author and publisher shall not be liable for misuse of this material. The purpose of this book is to educate and entertain. The author or publisher does not guarantee that anyone following these techniques, suggestions, tips, ideas, or strategies will become successful. The author or publisher shall have neither liability nor responsibility to anyone with respect to any loss of, damaged caused, or alleged to be caused, directly or indirectly by the information contained in this book.

Edited and Proofread by
Glenda Cody

Library of Congress Cataloging-in-Publication International Standard Book Number:2020909108

ISBN: 9781673169409

Printed in the United States of America.

DEDICATION

This book is dedicated to the Most High God, who has designed every aspect of my life. Through the pain, laughter, fear, anger, sadness, confusion, misunderstandings, disappointments, grief, celebrations, accomplishment, success, joy, and so much more, he continues to keep me. Therefore, I can share my story in hopes that it will reach my readers inspiring them and motivating them to continue to trust our Most High God. To my son, Charles, who was God's plan, who has saved my life. My son being only 12 years old has encouraged me in so many ways. I know the Lord speaks through you son. Continue to hold dear to Him. Allowing Him to be sovereign over your life. Never forget that you can call on His name at any time. There is power in the name of Jesus! I love you CJ!

To my family, who has been there from day one. My sister Tiyana Hunter and my brother Olliver Cody. Growing up we shared ups and downs. We grew apart at times, yet God has brought us together. We are now closer than ever before. I love you both dearly! I am so thankful to have both of you in my life. You are my support.

To my Mother, who did everything in her power to ensure my siblings and me were well taken care of. My mother shared love and laughter. She always provided a listening ear. She knew all my secrets. My mother knew my deep passion for writing. She would read my short stories and smile. She believed in me. During the times we did not see eye to eye, she always met me with love, right in the moment. I miss her so much and know she is smiling. She smiled each stroke of the keyboard during this project. That is how I was able to continue. I love you momma; you are my Angel.

To My Father, who has always showed tough love. Yet, made himself available in times of need. Though our relationship did not grow the way I felt it should, God still allowed us to relationship. Daddy you were a great example to me. You showed me what a hard-working man looks like. I admire you in so many ways. You have encouraged me and pushed me. I will never forget your words "walk in light." I love you daddy.

Isaiah 43:18-19 NIV
"Forget the former things; do not dwell on the past. See, I am doing a new thing!
Now it springs up; do you not perceive it? I am making a way in the wilderness and
streams in the wasteland.

Standing In God's Promises

Luke 15:3-7 NIV

Then Jesus told them this parable: "Suppose one of you has a hundred sheep and loses one of them. Doesn't he leave the ninety-nine in the open country and go after the lost sheep until he finds it? And when he finds it, he joyfully puts it on his shoulders and goes home. Then he calls his friends and neighbors together and says, 'Rejoice with me; I have found my lost sheep.' I tell you that in the same way there will be more rejoicing in heaven over one sinner who repents than over ninety-nine righteous persons who do not need to repent."

ACKNOWLEDGEMENT

Thank you to all who believed in me.

Introduction

As a child I always desired more for my life. Between the age of ten and fifteen, I assumed this feeling I felt; *the more* was becoming an Oscar winning actress. Or maybe a professional dancer. Maybe I would be America's Next Top Model. They say dream *big*. Children tend to be in tune with their inner self. There are no fears or hold backs. Children go for what they want. My thoughts as a child were centered around my desires as well as the world's. Dream big. What is dream big? I thought, as a child, big had to have a title. I thought for my accomplishment to carry weight, people had to see me. Yet, deep down inside I wanted to be in the background. I wanted the impact of whatever I did to be the big. In society today, your accolades, financial status, and popularity status is what defines your success. It does not matter what product you are selling nor the impact it has on people (good or bad). YOU matter. As an adult today, I do not agree with this. I also realize you, me, WE, do not matter at all. I realize God's will for our lives is how we are all connected. God's will for my life, even as a child, was the desire and the more. This is greater than some title. Far greater than just you and I alone as individuals. I have always had this feeling tugging at me, a voice whispering, *"there is more."* Growing up I knew there were more stairs to climb. As many breathes as I have there must be more. As a child I recall having all these creative ideas and talents. I was a free spirit. One day I would be writing a book and completing it and the next day I would be making a dance routine and teaching my childhood best friend. After rehearsing, repeatedly, we would perform in front of our friends and family. Isn't it amazing as children we allow our spirits to lead us without any hesitation? Just think about it. At times you may have believed you were a superhero with your cape tied around your neck. Or maybe you were a mother of five, who ensured dinner was prepared, the kitchen was clean, and your daughters' hair was combed. You rocked your children to sleep. For my male readers, I have just described us women as little girls playing with our dolls and being successful at exemplifying the characteristics of the Proverbs 31 virtuous women. Hope you got a laugh out of that.

As kids we do not care what other's think about our gifts, ideas nor imagination. In Kindergarten it came to me to write children books and sell them at school for 25 cents. I wanted to inspire at an early age. That drive has always been there. I recall putting together a group with some friends, where we only used Pig-Latin language. I completed the research on this language and began practicing writing the language. I taught a couple of friends and we all began to use Pig-Latin while writing letters to one another. It was so cool then! You know what, it is cool now also. We did not care what others thought. When an idea was placed inside, we acted on it in confidence. I like to call it an unknown faith.

What happens once we become young adults and then adults? Where does that drive go? Or, shall I ask where did *my* drive go? What caused me to stop believing? Better question, and the purpose of my story, what caused me to *start* believing? I have decided to share a piece of me. Share my trials and tribulations. Share how all along the Lord was in my life helping me along the way. Even at times when my ears and eyes were closed shut. As a child, He was there. As an adult, He was there. You know what? Even before I entered the womb, He **knew** me. What I want my readers to understand is, everything that has happened, is happening, or will happen, God is aware, was aware, and still is aware. He is the Most High God who is sovereign over all things. Good or bad. Ups or downs. Past, present, and future. He is IAM.

In my story, I share how one day my eyes and ears opened. I allowed Jesus Christ to enter my heart and my mind. I allowed the Lord to be sovereign over my life. Read my words, and I pray, you hear God's voice in the midst. I pray he speaks to you and you are willed to hear him clearly.

You may not realize it, but you are standing in God's promises.

CHAPTER 1

I remember my dad would pull up in that white pickup truck. That truck may have been old, but it was new to me every time I saw it. It was white and it was my daddy's truck. I knew every time I saw it; I was going on a ride. My dad would pull up in front of my mom's house just to take his baby girl on a ride around the block on the back of the pickup truck. This is how I remember it. Man, did I love this! I remember getting in the back of the pickup truck thinking "there are no seat belts. Oh well, I'm with my daddy. I will be just fine." I knew I was safe being with my daddy. It would be a nice summer day when my dad would pull up and put me in the back. Riding on the back I enjoyed the summer breeze. Of course, it was hot out, but the wind blowing would cool me down. I felt free. Cars would pull up behind us and I would smile and wave. I was content being with my dad. My dad also had a yellow Volvo. He would play the singer Brandy's tape cassette in his tape player in the car. *"Sittin Up in My Room."* I would sing along to my favorite song. My daddy knew that was my favorite song. I believe he would purposely play this song for me when I would be in the car. Maybe he liked the song as well or maybe he just wanted his baby girl to be happy as she sang along to her favorite song. Yep, those were the days. When the song would end, I would rewind the cassette to the beginning. I would play it over and over until it was time to get out of the car. The year of '95, when tape players were around, the white pickup truck, the Volvo, and my daddy. Special times in my life.

My household consisted of my older sister, brother, nephew, mother and me. I was around seven years old during this time. My family was your average family. We had times when we disagreed, we also had times when we got along well. We would attend church as a family every blue moon. I love my family dearly. At times I did have doubts on whether they loved me. Understand, I was the youngest of three, I was the baby. When questioning my family's love, I was always reassured that their love for me was real. I remember one year coming home from school. It was my birthday and I was anticipating the love. As I walked into the kitchen, I approached my sister and brother. My sister and brother acknowledged me, however, did not mention anything about a birthday. MY Birthday. Instead my sister said, "Hey, how was school? Take your things upstairs so we can get ready for dinner." I walked upstairs wondering why they had not acknowledged my birthday.

"They don't love me." I said aloud to myself as I placed my things in my room. I washed my hands and returned to the kitchen. Immediately my heart filled with so much joy. I looked at my sister who was wearing a beautiful smile. My brother wore the same smile. "Happy Birthdaaaaay!" They both yelled. They came and hugged me, and I returned the love. I blew out candles on a cake which was set out on the table surrounded by balloons, gifts, and most important, my family.

"You two tricked me!" I yelled back, feeling special. My family did love me after all. So, as you see, love was important in our household. It did not go unnoticed. My mother worked two jobs to support her three children. She also attended community college to earn her associate degree in social work in hopes to better support her family. My mother made many sacrifices for her children. There was a time my mother arrived home with brand new bedroom furniture for my brother and me. My sister was moved out at this time. My brother and I were so happy about our new bedroom sets. This was not bad for a single mother during these times. My mother set up our bedroom sets in our rooms. As I entered my bedroom, I fixed my eyes on the beautiful white bed post. I felt like a princess. My mother also installed carpet in our rooms. Brand new carpet. Our rooms were well put together. The walls in my room were white with a floral border. I enjoyed walking barefoot in my room. My small feet would seep into the thick soft carpet. My mother also purchased me a white vanity, where I could sit and play in makeup. We found so much gratitude in the way our mother showed us love.

There were so many other things our family received from my mother. Holidays were the best! When Christmas Eve arrived, we all dwelled in our anxiety and excitement. Not wanting to fall asleep because we did not want to miss anything. So instead, we stayed up to feed our excitement. We watched Christmas traditions such as Rudolph and Jack Frost. Our mother allowed us to open one present on Christmas Eve night. We all gathered around the beautiful Christmas tree. Smelling the fresh pine. I remember there being so many gifts under the Christmas tree. My brother and I were able to hang our ornaments, we made at school, on the Christmas tree. Traditional white lights were my mom's favorite. My nephew and I would dig into the popcorn can that my mom provided each Christmas. We would make our way through each flavor, cheddar, white cheddar, and caramel. We would all fall asleep and wake up the next morning to enjoy a beautiful Christmas day with our family.

Waking up on Christmas day we would quickly open our gifts. Our mother prepared a big breakfast, we all sat around in excitement. Enjoying tearing through all our gifts to see the gift we had seen either from a commercial or maybe while in a department store as our mother shopped. Having those toys in our hands, in our home, was truly a blessing for us. Our mother made it happen. It didn't stop there. My mother's love was for everyone.

We would have cookouts that my mother would host. She planned family reunions. Inviting aunts, uncles, cousins, and all the family. We would all sit back enjoying the music and the good food. We would play games at the family reunion from volleyball to washers. Man, these were the good times. My mother was very family oriented. She loved her family.

Memory

My sheep hear my voice, and I know them, and they follow me: John 10:27 KJV

One of the best things I received from my mother as a child, was a children's bible. I am sure it was passed down from my sister, to my brother, and finally me. I read the stories and studied the pictures in the book. I may have been around eight or nine years old. As I read the book, I felt the desire to know more about our God. My mother took us to church, and we would enjoy service and return home for Sunday dinner. There were some occasions when I would go to church with my cousins. I will never forget a special day I attended church with my cousins. All the teenagers were called to the alter for prayer. While this was going on, I really did not understand the purpose. I didn't understand why the teenagers were being called to the alter. Keep in mind, I did not attend church regularly with my family. I went down to the alter with my cousins. A woman approached me and began to pray. When she finished her prayer, she began to speak. She said some things along the line of fleeing from worldly acts. She used the term "fast" in reference to living a fast life. Growing up too fast, partaking in adult activities. I began to cry. This woman did not know me, yet her words pierced. As I cried, I didn't understand why I cried. Today, I understand I was releasing things deep down inside which I hadn't identified because of shame. In that moment, walls were being broken down.

I had partaken in things which I knew were inappropriate for me. By the age of thirteen I found a way to porn. Porn led to my curiosity of sex. At this time in my life I had no idea what I was headed for. In the moment when the woman spoke to me at the church and the walls began to fall, I let out a cry to the Lord. I remember calling up on his name. Jesus! The Holy Spirit moved me! I lost control of my body as well as my tongue. I sent praises to the Most High God. I was not a member of this church, but God *still* spoke to me. I did not attend that church, nor any other church regularly. Yet God; the Most High God spoke to me. Halleluiah! God will meet you anywhere! We must have a posture to receive. This God, who I had read about in my children's bible some years ago, met me at that church in that hour. That hour was ordained by God. I allowed the words the woman spoke to me to enter my heart. She didn't know me; but God did. She was his vessel. Some may call what I am describing an emotional experience. I beg to differ. I encountered an experience with Glory! Yes, emotion was preset, my tears. However, I had never experienced anything like this, during other emotional experiences I'd encountered. There was a movement on the inside.

That little girl on the inside had gotten a glimpse of someone near who was coming to save her. She began to chase after that glimpse. Soon the cries turned into praise. The girl was loosed! She was free! After this, I returned to my cousin's home that night and documented the events which took place that day in my journal. That night I kept wondering, why did this affect me this way? Why me? I was in awe! I knew there was a God; I'd experienced divine intervention. That lady had no idea of what doors I'd opened. God spoke a word to her, and she acted out of obedience. Little did I know, there was so much more to come. The Lord had come after His lost sheep. I knew his voice.

Chapter 2

I lost my virginity at the age of thirteen. Talk about a fast life. I really do not feel great about admitting that I was sexually active at the age of thirteen. However, I am not the first nor the last. I am also a witness that our Most High God loves us where we are. Despite what the folks in your church home may think of you, or that family member who doesn't know your story, and judges you. God knows your story.

My first year in high school I decided to allow a boy I liked at the time; and dated, to take my virginity. Though I participated in the act; I never viewed myself as fast. Then I did not know it, but I was seeking something that I felt I did not have. I decided to use sex as an outlet. The close males in my family at the time were away or distant. My brother had gone off to join the Navy and my father; well he was newly married.

When my father became married things changed. Our relationship changed. I would see my dad less frequently. There were things I feel I should have been taught by my father. Values and self-worth. My father and I never discussed the possibilities of myself and a young man. We never discussed my value. You know, words of affirmation. My father has never told me I was beautiful. My dad never really shared how he felt about me nor thought of me. Words of affirmation is one of my love languages. I'm not blaming my dad for my choice to lose my virginity at thirteen; however, as an adult I do feel it is very important for a father to instill certain values and morals into his children. This is important for both sons and daughters.

As a teenager I focused on boys. Boys that I liked. I was not promiscuous. There were only two boys at the time; one broke my heart; and the other took my virginity. I just gave my precious treasure away. I had no business acting out this way. I should have focused on school and school only. See, we can't just say that's the resolution. We all have our own journey. We will make mistakes. Again, I am sharing to be a witness that during that time when I was sexually active at the age of thirteen and feeling rejected by my father; I was standing in God's Promises. Hope you're following me.....

Of course, I encourage my young adult readers to hold off on becoming sexually active. However, I will say things do not always take place in the perfect order. So, my true purpose and goal is to show my readers that when we are out of order, we have a God who walks with us, protects us, and continues to keep us through our journey. Soon to bring us into order. To my young adult readers, if you feel you are being peer pressured, to do things which you know are inappropriate, talk to your parents about it. Refrain from talking to friends. Instead, you need wisdom, you need direction. I spoke with friends about my desires and curiosity. I avoided speaking with my parents. That was not the right thing to do.

A Daughter's Resentment

When my father married things changed as I mentioned before. The treatment I received made me resent my father's marriage. Those truck rides were over. Maybe because we were not in the year of '95. I had become older. However, I do not feel at the age of eight a little girl shouldn't be a princess any longer. My loss of virginity was at the age of thirteen, but I feel my relationship with my father was cut off between the age of eight and ten.

I can recall reaching out to my dad, and him always saying "Hey! I have to give you a call back." The phone would disconnect. This became repetitive. Other times I would get the voicemail. Rejection. I was being rejected, by my own dad. Why doesn't he want to talk to me? I would ask myself. I continued to live wondering why my dad no longer shared a relationship me. Yet, I would still attempt to call. I didn't realize this chase after my father was only the beginning of a behavior that would last for a very long time. The chase.

This carried on for years. I began to believe it was normal. I decided to place my dad upon a shelf. I began to find interest in boys by the time I got into high school. A friend of mine encouraged me to become intimate with the guy I was dating. I don't like to say I was peer pressured. Though in reality, I was. The ultimate choice to follow through on what my friend had proposed was my decision, and my desire. I noticed the seed, which was planted so many years back, when I had begun to watch porn. The curiosity developed and now actions were taking place.

After losing my virginity I was not intimate again until my junior year in high school. By my junior year in high school I was sexually active. I had become what I thought was a "woman." My mother could sense it.

Chapter 3

My mom was worried about me. I would hear my mother on the telephone with her friends expressing concerns for my changed behavior. What my mom may not have known, is the cloud that hung heavy over my head. The perception of my father not cherishing me. I would watch my friends and their fathers and see how they would interact with one another. I would watch television shows and see how a father cherished his daughter. Why was my relationship so different with mine?

My mother was able to identify with her seed. There goes that love. She sensed something. I couldn't bring myself to confess to my mom the things I'd partaken in. Sex. I was ashamed. I chose to hold it all in. Me being intimate, as well as being hurt. It was my little secret. As I held it in; I released and escaped through sex. I wanted to let my mom know the truth, after I imagined her hugging me and not passing judgement. My fear was that I would be judged. My fear was that the trust between my mother and I would be broken. I could always remember being judged by others on the outside. Walking into a room; without anyone knowing my story; yet their stares and whispers stayed with me. I needed my mother to view me as her little girl. Really, during that time that is exactly what I was. A lost little girl. Wearing my big hoop earrings, blonde extensions, and make up. I did not want my mother to view me as the world viewed me. I didn't know what my dad saw me as. I needed reassurance from my mom. Sometimes, God permit things to happen to us, for us to better understand his love toward us. God works through those around us, through love.

I became pregnant at the age of sixteen. It was my senior year of high school. What was I thinking? I mean I'd heard stories of young girls becoming pregnant during high school. I always told myself that wouldn't be me. Well it was. I was devastated when I found out I was pregnant. My mother cried and asked why I'd lied to her. My mother had inquired with me on numerous occasions if I was sexually active. I couldn't bring myself to honesty. Well the truth always comes out. I sat in the car as the doctor waited for our response and reaction after he shared the news.

My mom and I arrived at the doctor's office for a wellness check. My mother requested that I provide a urine sample to confirm if I was pregnant. When I heard her request this I felt as though my life had frozen. Everything was still. I began to think back to vomiting during class just a week ago, and my missed period. I knew I was pregnant. How did she know? I attempted to stall explaining to my mother and doctor that I did not have to urinate. Isn't it something how as kids and young adults we know nothing? We only think for the moment. Was I planning to just "hide" my pregnancy for 10 months? They were both incredibly supportive by bringing me cups of water. There was no way I was getting out of this! I drank the cups of water, and really needed to urinate. The doctor took the sample and asked us to wait for results. We'd been at the doctor's office the entire morning, and it was crowded. My mother decided we would run to get food and asked the lady at the front desk if she could phone us the results. I don't know why I assumed I was free, and my little secret would remain my little secret in a urine cup. I guess in that moment I was just happy to be out of that place. We ordered our food and received our order. We walked to the car to drive off to head home, and something taps on the passenger side window. I look up to see my doctor.

Chapter 4

Oh no. My face froze. The results were back. My mother rolled down her window. The doctor's office and food place were in the same plaza. How did this man, the doctor, just run out of his office across the parking lot to my mother's vehicle? How did he even know what vehicle we were in?

"I have the results back, Ms. Hunter.... would you like to come into my office, or I can share here?"

"She's pregnant isn't she!?" My mother said with a mixture of frustration and confirmation. I immediately began to cry as I looked into the doctor's eyes.

"Yes, she is. We have options if you're not planning to carry to term." It's like he immediately went to those options because of how young I was. I mean, I was only sixteen years old. What was I thinking? I wasn't. My mother advised the doctor that she would give him a call. As we rode home my mom asked one question.

"Precious, why did you lie to me?" Her voice had so much disappointment in it. It's like she found it so hard to believe that I had been lying to her. Yet, she wasn't upset. She was hurt. Seeing how hurt and disappointed she was, hurt me. I had let my mother down. My mother was a great mother and was a mother who you could talk to. I allowed myself to be distant from her. Instead of leaning to her in a time of need. I never answered my mother's question. I only cried and responded by saying "I'm sorry." I was truly sorry. I was sorry for keeping secrets. I was sorry for breaking the trust we had. I was sorry for letting her down. I was sorry for going against everything she'd taught me. I was sorry.

When we arrived home, my mom didn't yell at me. She did not call me names. She did not judge me. As I cried, she reassured me that she was here to support me through this. She allowed me to decide what I wanted to do with my body. She did not force me to do anything. My God! The Lord worked through my mother. Unconditional Love. My mother could have easily written me off. She didn't.

You may be judging. You may say what you would have done. Let me ask; has God forgiven you today? Is He still a provider? Is he still Jehovah Rapha? My mother did not allow this circumstance to bring her out of love. She parented through love and sought God for direction. My mom could have *made* me have my child, or she could have *made* me abort my child. I decided to abort my child, at the age of sixteen. I was not ready. This was very selfish of me and I know what you're thinking. If I could engage in adult behavior, then I should be able to handle the responsibility of parenting. I couldn't. I was not ready to do what I knew nothing about.

Chapter 5

My mother did not want me to go through with the abortion.

"I can't believe I am going to let you do this to my grandbaby." Even in her doubt as a parent, who at any moment could take full control of the situation and say, "No. You are going to take care of your responsibility." She did not. She must have hurt quietly. As I reflect on the decision I made then; today, I know I made that decision based on what others would think or say. I was also fearful of becoming a mother. I did not regret it when I made the decision. During that time, I never wondered "what if"? The decision I made did not affect me mentally nor emotionally, so I thought. I just wanted to be a kid again.

My father never knew about this incident. I don't believe he did. However, I do recall a year later, in 2007, my dad called and said "So your pregnant huh? Your uncle told me." It was funny because, my dad never really called. When I would attempt to call him, he would either rush me off the phone, or not answer. Now I had an incoming call from him. That was a horrible and surprising way for him to find out. I ended up pregnant a year later. Yep, I continued to engage in sexual activities after my first abortion. I know as you're reading, you're trying to keep up. Remember the woman from church service who ministered to me? She attempted to pray me away from the fast life. However, I had to go through my journey. What was revealed is God is real. Yet, we still have our journeys to take. Just know He's with you every step of the way. I was thirteen when the woman ministered to me at Lively Stone church. I was now nineteen and pregnant for the second time. I didn't choose obedience even after receiving that powerful word. I chose to continue to do things my way. Yet, I was still standing in God's Promises. My life was about to change drastically. Something was taking place that I would have never imagined. Life was being birthed; and life was passing on.

Memory

I remember sitting in the bathtub, talking to a friend who was away at college. My friend had just shared with me devastating news about one of our high school classmates. Her mother had passed away. I felt so bad and sent condolences. I said to my friend "I am so sorry to hear this! Man, I wouldn't know what to do if my mother left here." Little did I know, she was already being positioned to leave, as I spoke those words.

Before I found out I was pregnant, the second time, I went to the hospital to visit my mother. She had been in and out of the hospital a lot lately. My siblings and I did not fully understand why. During that time, I was too selfish to even try to begin to understand why. I had just graduated from high school and received my first credit card. I wanted to share the exciting news with my mom. I went into the hospital room and shared the news. I was approved for my first credit card. I can recall my uncle being in the room with us. I rambled on and on until my mother said "Baby I have to tell you something. I have cancer." Blank. I can't remember my response, I can't remember anything after she said that but, blank. I do remember running away from the fact that my mother was diagnosed with lymphoma cancer. Cancer? No not cancer, not my mother! This went on for a while. The back and forth in my mind, knowing reality but finding a box to store more issues next to my daddy issues, on my secret shelves. As I closed the box, I sealed it with; my mother will be just fine, she is strong and always pulls through.

Finding out my mother was diagnosed with cancer was something I did not want to accept. I figured if I continued to go through life normal, everything would come back together as normal. My mother would be free of cancer. I avoided reality. It's like I wanted to become apathetic to the situation just to avoid the fact that my mother really had cancer. My aunt would provide me with brochures to better understand the type of cancer as well as how to cope with having a parent who was diagnosed with cancer. The pamphlet also explained how to be there for support. I would become so angry reading those pamphlets. Why is this happening with my family, my mother? She has been the best mother, sister, aunt, cousin, friend, why is this happening? Those thoughts constantly ran in my head.

I visited my mother one day to spend some time with her. As I walked into my mom's bedroom, I saw her lying in bed with a scarf on. Her friend sat on the opposite end of the bed. I greeted my mother's friend as he moved to allow me to sit closer to my mom. My mom smiled and asked how I was doing. See, she was always concerned about someone else. God why did she have to go through this? I remember bypassing my mom's question and asked how she was doing. She smiled and said she couldn't complain. She then removed her scarf from her head. My mother's hair had fallen out from the chemotherapy. I cried. I laid my head on my mom and cried. She caressed me as she cried. Even during her trials, she nurtured. I know, as a mother, she wanted the pain to go away within. As a daughter I wanted the pain, the sickness, and the fear to go away from my mother. I wanted my mother to have her life back. We laid there and cried. My mom's friend stepped out of the room. My heart hurt so bad. As I write my heart hurts. To see my mother in that state broke my spirit. My heart was broken. Life was supposed to remain the same, this was NOT supposed to take place.

Chapter 6

My mother remained in and out of the hospital. I would visit my mom during my lunch breaks. I would give my mom foot rubs as she would encourage me to live healthy. Being mindful of the foods I ate and committing to exercise. She always would warn me to never try any drug. My mom always educated. I remember when I was fifteen years old, we went to Commerce Bank to open a savings and checking account. She also taught me how to balance a checkbook. As we would talk in those hospital rooms, I couldn't help but to keep in the back of mind that she was sick. As much as I wanted to enjoy the moment, I couldn't. I was hurt. I was upset.

One day I picked up the telephone to call my mom. She was at home at that time. One year after I graduated from high school, I learned I was pregnant. This was the second pregnancy. I cried as I shared the news with her. I cried because I was ashamed. I had just had an abortion the year before and I was pregnant again.

"Why are you crying? Don't you know you're going to be okay?" My mom's voice was full of peace. However, I could also hear the exhaustion in her tone. The exhaustion of fighting a battle of illness. "You have nothing to worry about, stop crying. You will be just fine. It will be just fine. I love you." As I listened on the other end of the phone, my tears slowed down. My heart began to beat normal. My mother calmed me. She spoke with so much confidence and reassurance. It's like my mom had received the confirmation that CJ and I would be okay. I made the decision in that moment to carry out my pregnancy.

Chapter 7

My mother passed away on November 23, 2007. I received a phone call from my sister who was at the hospital. It was early in the morning. The night before I had managed to sleep through the entire night. I had been having a hard time sleeping before. As my sister cried over the phone making me aware that my mom had passed away, my physical, mental and spiritual being went weak. I dropped the phone and fell back onto the bed. I let out a cry, that I didn't know exist. I screamed. My son's father came running in. I could barely let out what was wrong. He had to assist me with getting clothes on to make our way to the hospital. As we pulled into the parking garage at the hospital, the security officer assisted as my son's dad tried to get me to walk into the hospital. They managed to get me in. I walked into the room my mother was in. I walked in to see my mother laying there as if she was sleeping. It hurt like hell to know she was not sleeping. I walked over to my mom and laid my head on her thigh. I grabbed her hand and caressed them as I cried. She didn't caress me back. JESUS! My momma was gone! I could hear my sister crying and screaming. My dad entered the room. I cannot recall if I called my dad or if my sister called my dad. My brother had to receive the news over a payphone. He managed to walk to a payphone that morning and call my sister's cell phone. He made his way to the hospital. It breaks my heart when I think about my brother and his story. My brother joined the Navy and returned home to care for my mother. He was away for maybe 2-3 years and when he returned home, our mother was passing away. I love you brother.

We all gathered around, laying in tears, sadness, anger, disbelief and grief. Our mother was just here with us. She attended my high school graduation in 2006 and passed away a year later. I never imagined this would be my life. My mother was 50 years old when she passed away.

I tried to wrap my mind around what had just taken place. She was no longer here on earth. Today I still have not wrapped my mind around this. You know, I have my days. I have my days when I'm strong in resting in God's peace. Other days I continue to rest in peace as he allows me to be a daughter who misses her momma. Thank you, Lord, for allowing me to be human. Allowing me to grieve. My mother was a beautiful person. I can recall her laughing with her head tilted back. She was filled with so much joy and love. I continued to struggle with the fact that I would never get to see her again. I wouldn't talk to her or touch her. I couldn't hug her. My world was upside down. The day of the funeral I was numb. That same "blank" affect took affect the day of my mom's funeral. People approached me but I can't recall faces. As I walked up to the casket that my mother laid in, I kissed her cheek. The feeling of her cheek hurt me so bad. There was no life. I was only kissing the outer shell. Tears fell down my face, as anger filled me. I could hear my sister's screams. "I just want my momma! Momma please!" Lord knows I couldn't take it! My heart began to race! The little being inside of me never moved, nor fluttered. I am sure my emotions overtook his movements. I took a seat on the church pew next to my aunt. I could feel my aunt's sorrow. During the days my mother was ill, my aunt was by my mom's side. Assisting her in every way needed. My aunt cared for her sister. Her little sister. To lose a sister must have been heartbreaking. Everyone hurt that day. My mother, our mother, a sister, an aunt, a cousin, a faithful friend, had gone away. She was no longer with us; physically.

At the burial I felt a tap on my shoulder. I turned to see my dad and stepmother. They both gave me a hug and told me they would be leaving town that day to complete a business deal. I didn't feel anything when I heard the news. To be honest, in that moment, to even question *why* my father was not staying with my brother and I to support, was impossible. I heard him and responded "okay." After the burial family and friends gathered at my sister's house. I went into a room on the second level to get away from everything and everyone. I laid there and rubbed my belly. The little baby inside still hadn't fluttered. I prayed that I would fall into a deep sleep. I struggled with falling asleep. I could only think about my mother being gone and my son not getting the chance to meet his grandmother. Suddenly I felt a flutter.

Chapter 8

On March 23, 2008 I gave birth to my son. He was 7.6 lbs. and 21 inches. A healthy baby despite the things we had gone through. I must say labor was a piece of work! I endured so much pain as I pushed, pushed and pushed. Finally, at 11:57pm exact, the little prince arrived. "I wish my mommy was here!" I said to my sister and my son's father. My mother told me while she was in the hospital, a few weeks before she passed away, that I would have a son. The Lord revealed this to my mother while she was still here on Earth. It came to pass. While I was pregnant, I prayed for a son. *"For this child I prayed; and the Lord hath given me my petition which asked of him."* 1 Samuel 1:27 NIV

After giving birth I stayed in the hospital for three days. My sister, my son's father, his mother, a couple of friends, and my stepsister came to visit me and my new baby at the hospital. I was thankful to have them there. I didn't receive cards nor balloons, the hospital room appeared to be empty. However, this was a new beginning. My baby boy was here, and my mother was aware of this before she left. Today I understand the peace she carried. God's peace. I know my mother had been talking to God before leaving Earth. I know she had prayed for her children. I know she prayed for the Lord to cover us. That He did and continues to do today.

As I laid in the hospital, I realized I was dealing with mixed emotions. I was thrilled to have my child, yet still grieving. I laid in bed thinking, as my son's father and mother inquired the name of our child. I decided to name my son after his father. We call him CJ. When it was time to leave the hospital it's like "mommy mode" went into full effect. I must be honest as we prepared CJ's car seat with the assistance of one of the nurses, I thought to myself, "What in the world now?" I knew the nurse couldn't hop in the car and go home with us to show me how to parent. I knew I must protect, care, and most important love this little boy. I sat in the back seat watching my baby boy's little eyes wonder. I reassured him. The same way my mom always reassured me. I whispered to him "I will not fail you; I love you." I kissed him on his little cheek and watched him fall asleep.

We arrived home and I immediately cared, protected, and loved on my baby. I surprised myself! I was pumping milk, storing bags, referencing dates and times on freezer bags to know the accurate time which the milk was pumped and stored. I created a chart to capture feeding times. When I was pregnant with him, I would read to him and this continued once we settled home. I would also sing to my son. I was a mother. I enjoyed these special moments. There were times I would watch my son play with the air. He would move his little small hand in the air as if he were trying to touch or grab something. He would laugh and smile. I know to this day; my Angel came to visit. We love you momma.

Chapter 9

My son's father and I shared great moments as we parented together. We also experienced challenges during my pregnancy, while my mother was passing, as well as after my pregnancy. There was a time, while I was pregnant, I had just gotten off work and wanted to grab something to eat out before heading home. Normally I would eat a home cooked meal. After grabbing something to eat and heading back home I spotted my son's father. As I looked in his car it appeared to be another male in the car. I assumed this was the case, why would there be a woman in the car? I quickly learned my assumptions were wrong. There was a young woman in the car. I pulled my car into the grocery store's parking lot where I spotted his vehicle. He approached my car once he had noticed I had pulled alongside of him. He reassured me the young lady was one of his friend's little sister. I knew he was lying. I was four months pregnant at the time and couldn't believe what was happening. He went back to his car and drove off. Oh no, he was not going to get away with this. I thought as I followed closely behind him. His car began to speed up. My car began to speed up. Before you knew it, we were in action. The smell of tires burning filled the air. We cut through stop signs and red lights, as he ran, and I chased. As I realized, the only reason I was four months pregnant and chasing the father of my child, who had another woman in the car with him, was because he was lying and obviously cheating. I decided to give up and go home. Its like a light bulb went off. I went home, took a hot bath, enjoyed my dinner, and cried myself to sleep.

There were many nights he would not come home. We were not married, so home really was not home. We were fornicating. We lived a young wildlife. We would hang out at clubs, drink alcohol, and was unaware of the risk we took each night we did this. Thinking back, we were kids. During those days, I never thought about salvation much. Maybe never. However, I desired to know Jesus. That desire for more rose each night I would sit in somebody's club, and each night I was intimate with my son's father.

The next couple of years would result in betrayal, abuse, more alcohol, fornication and neglect. I was between the age of twenty and twenty-two. I will admit, I enjoyed hanging out in clubs, though that voice would nag me. Telling me I should not be there. I began drinking once my mother passed. I would drink to the point of blacking out. I was a mother by day, and a twenty-one-year-old by night. At that time, I released a lot of the pain I held within from losing my mother, as well as feeling abandoned by my father. Those two boxes remained on my secret shelves. I would drink to forget the boxes even existed. During this time, I thought the wildlife was the thing to do. I would wear little to nothing to clubs. I didn't have anyone close to me telling me otherwise. This reminds me of the scripture *"But Jesus said unto him, follow me; and let the dead bury the dead." Matthew 8:22 KJV.* During those times I never came across this scripture, however, I would hear His voice. As I would sit in those nightclubs the voice would tell me that some of those people were spiritually dead, including myself. I was not there to just have a good time. I was lost. I was coping. I was dependent upon things which were not helping nor healing me. Spiritually dead. I didn't have any awareness of who I was. I needed to leave that lifestyle alone.

I knew I didn't *fit in.* I knew I had no business partaking in the things which I did. I ignored the voice time and time again. I felt as though at that time, I didn't have any role models in my life. No one was there who could recognize my attempt to cope with grief by self-destruction. Someone could have said "you have a baby for crying out loud!" Nope, everyone I was with, was on the same agenda. I must say, I was not a bad parent by far, however, I partied way too much. I continued to party and fornicate. There would be some nights I would stay in the clubs until 6am, leave and drop friends off at work. Today, you can't get me to stay up past 10pm. You're probably wondering where would my little one be when I was out. He would be cared for by his grandmother. My son's father's mom.

Chapter 10

Before having my son, my son's father and I became distant once I moved into my first apartment. He noticed I was not paying him much attention. Once he realized this, I became pregnant by him. No worries, God's Plan. I will share, he did confess to purposely attempting to get me pregnant. Little did he know, God had been in control the entire time. Yes, there was a purpose. I do not blame my son's father for any of our challenges. We were both young. I have found it in my heart to forgive him for all things.

There were times, before I became pregnant as well as after, when we would fight. I recall a time we sat in my living room, with one of my cousins. We all listened to music, and shared laughter. My son's father stood up to announce he was running to the car to grab more CD's. He left out and never returned. I became curious and looked out the window. My car was missing. He had taken my vehicle. This was the first time he'd taken my vehicle. Earlier that evening he inquired if he could use my car. I told him no, knowing he did not have a valid driver's license. My son was born at this time, and I understood how important transportation was for myself and my child. My son's father did not understand. My insides began to boil as I dialed his cellphone and continued to be sent to the voicemail. I was furious! I began to form resentment toward him. I was tired of being mistreated. To take something of mine, that I worked hard for, put us in a different place. I continued to allow him to live with me, which opened doors for more things to take place. God was always in the midst whispering to me *"you're worth so much more."*

Chapter 11

Standing in God's Promises

I am with you and will watch over you wherever you go, and I will bring you back to this land. I will not leave you until I have done what I have promised you.

Genesis 28:15

I would always sit back and wonder where all the mistreatment came from that I endured. From my father, my son's father, and people in general. I knew I carried integrity. I always had good intentions. Even when being done wrong. So why did I have to endure so much? As I would reflect on my relationship, I could not understand why the person I had grown to love and care for, would want to hurt me. He was really my escape. So, I thought. One night, the ambulance was called. He wanted to use my car, and I said no. He needed to take his friend home. We had talks about this before and agreed anytime his friends came over, they would need to have a way home. Why did I need to tell him this? Hearing me say no, made him upset. He grabbed me and began to strangle me. I am not sure what had come over him, but he had become physically abusive. He placed his knees on my neck and jammed his knees into my neck. We were in a corner in my bedroom, as my child, who was between 4-6 months laid in bed crying. His friend watched. He did not intervene. Who would save me? I did not recognize this place! Abuse! I felt helpless, and lifeless. My asthma began to flare up. Once he noticed how weak I had become, he removed his knees from my neck and his hands from my hands. He held my hands with his hands to prevent me from being able to fight back. He got up and snatched my car keys. He and his friend left in my car. I was able to gather myself and run to a friend's home. Out of panic, I grabbed my son who was dressed in a onesie and no socks. I threw a blanket around him and rushed out. It was very cold outside. I worried and prayed that my baby wouldn't become ill. We were able to contact the authorities, and reported my car missing.

There were many times like these before I found the courage to walk away. You are probably thinking, wow that wasn't enough? Nope, for some reason it was not. I remained in a relationship. I ended up getting a restraining order on my son's father. I began to fear my wellbeing. I had no idea what had taken place. What made him become so abusive? I arrived home one day once he and I decided to go our separate ways. He was in my home, hiding under my bed. Sounds creepy right? It was. So, I was sure to get a restraining order. My son's father and I shared mutual friends. Some felt that

I over exaggerated the dysfunction and abuse. I mean, if I didn't want to except that I was in an abusive relationship, I could have remained, and just called our situation dysfunctional. Nope, that wasn't going to happen. I called it what it was. If it quacks like a duck, it's a duck. I never wanted any of this to happen. I cared for him deeply. For heaven sakes, he's the father of my child. No woman *wants* to take these kinds of precautions.

I began to attempt to date other men, once I got out of that relationship. Some of my friends, at the time would say, "Girl that is your son's father. How are you going to do him like that?" Disbelief! I may have done some foolish things, but I had common sense. Hell, I wanted to live! I also wanted to live outside of a cell. Someone could have gotten seriously hurt. I had to put an end to this! I didn't owe anyone an explanation. I let the dead bury the dead. All the back lash, all the false accusations, and opinions, I let it be! I clung to the Lord's words *"you're worth so much more."*

After getting the restraining order, things began to simmer down. I was no longer being threatened, verbally, nor physically abused by my son's father. He was no longer popping up in my back yard to control who I dated. He was no longer running away my guy friends. His lifestyle became more toxic, without me being apart of it. He began to drink more. We would drink while we were together as well. It seemed the alcohol had a different affect on him. My son's grandmother stepped in fully. She has been a great support from day one. I am truly thankful the Lord has allowed her to be my son's grandmother. We all continued to pray for my son's father. We prayed he would recover and become the father we all knew he could be. Over time, my son's father and I decided to co-parent. All things don't last forever. My son has a great relationship with his father. I have also forgiven him for the mistreatment. I pray he has forgiven himself as well.

Chapter 12

If we confess our sins, he is faithful and just to forgive us our sins, and to cleanse us from all unrighteous. 1 John 1:9 KJV

After I went through the ups and downs with my son's father. We separated for good. My son's grandmother and I began to build a relationship through caring for my son together. My mother had passed away, and I did not have much support. God again, knew exactly where we were and what we needed. I was single and decided to reconnect with an old friend. He was away in college, and I was in a relationship with my son's father. By the time he came back between 2008 and 2009, we began to spend time with one another. My friend and I dated on and off during high school. I had always had so much love for him. Yet, couldn't bring myself to be myself around him. It was weird. It's like I liked him so much, I would become frozen when we were around one another. Red flag #1. You should always be able to be yourself. I did not care about flags back then, I just wanted love.

I was so happy to have him back into my life. It was like a movie! He came back! He was my answer and my new beginning. Though so much time had passed while he was away, I still missed and loved him. We were still incredibly young and had no idea what we were doing with one another. I

41

was craving quality time, attention, and affection. We both had changed. I was trying to heal, yet still grieving. As people, we must learn to take time to ourselves. Trauma is real. We should not handle it lightly. I handled it lightly and jumped into a new relationship. Soon, I was doing the same things I had done in the last relationship. Drinking and fornicating. To be honest, I never stopped consuming alcohol. I suppressed my emotions with alcohol. I jumped into a relationship thinking all my hurt would go away. We would go out on dates and have drinks. To return home, to drink some more. So, was he *really* the answer? Was he *really* a new beginning? Sounds like the same problem and chapter to me.

He would often bring up marriage. When he would bring that word up; to be honest I took him as a joke. He had only been back in my lif a couple of months. My father had not met him. How could we just go and get married? It shocked many of my friends that I didn't shout yes as soon as he mentioned marriage. I was head over hills for this man, well, young man, while we were in school. It's like once the time presented itself, I didn't jump on it. Something just didn't feel right. Everything felt so rushed. I guess he was doing the right thing by trying to make me his wife. It just felt forced to me. I didn't want forced. We had chemistry, but nothing more. Or maybe I would not allow it to blossom. We had known each other for so long, yet really did not know each other. There were times when we would go days without speaking to one another, while in this relationship. I

42

did not have the patience for that type of behavior. I discovered he was

spending time with another woman, who he'd proposed to. Shortly after

that, I discovered a positive pregnancy test. Yep, I was pregnant.

My son was around two years old. I could not believe I had done this

again. Pregnant by someone, I was not sure of a long commitment with. I

had faced so many problems, my mind was boggled. At the time I learned I

was pregnant, the guy I dated shared he did not want to carry on a

relationship with me. He was in a relationship with someone else. He did

not want to attempt to reconnect. He continued a new relationship with the

woman I'd learned of during our relationship. Everything happened so fast.

I continued to think about what my father would say. He would be so

disappointed. It amazed me how I always thought about what my dad

would think. My dad was still in my life, at times. It was like pulling teeth to

get him to be a part of my life. He had come over a few times to visit me

and my son. He had even come over to house sit when my son's father and

I separated. At times I struggled financially. It was like pulling teeth to get

my dad to help me in times of need. All of this ran through my mind, as I

had to decide on bringing another child into the world. I didn't want to

struggle nor suffer anymore. My son and I alone, were already in a tight

position. Bringing another child into the world at that time, in my mind,

would only be more challenging. I made the decision to end my pregnanc

Chapter 13

"When my father and mother forsake me, then the Lord will take me up."

Psalm 27:10

I ended my pregnancy and became pregnant a second time by the same person. I ended that pregnancy as well. I had become so overwhelmed with everything; I fell into depression. I was already consuming alcohol to suppress emotions. I also began to spend money carelessly, avoided paying bills, dropped out of college, and at one point of time, stopped working. I stopped working for a short time. We still needed to eat. It's like I became so tired of having to be responsible. I felt as though I had too much on my plate. I was tired of parenting alone. My son's grandmother was a great support. Financially, it was just me. Money and time were running out. I eventually received an eviction notice on my front door. I didn't care. I was summoned to appear in court to care for past due payments. I was exhausted. The past three years in my first apartment had been a roller coaster. It was a party place. My friends would come over to drink and hang out. Once I had my son, we were sure to only party when he was away. However, this was supposed to be home. It should have had a settled tone. Instead it was loud. There were so many arguments and fights in that place. So many bad memories. The walls were decorated in depression. It was time for me to change scenery. I attended court and agreed to a payment plan to pay off the past due balance owed on the rent. I was not able to keep the commitment at that time.

The only person I could go to was my dad. I had hit rock bottom and did not know how to pick myself back up. I had nothing. I knew my son and I could not live on the streets. I felt as though I had failed as my dad began to yell at me for being so irresponsible. He didn't understand, I knew I was being irresponsible, I was tired of being responsible. I needed assistance, that was it. A little boost. A little direction. I didn't need boys, sex, alcohol, or clubs. I needed a father. It was well overdue. He was not happy about this at all. I can remember my dad always trying to explain to me that he was married now. He would say things were different. He would always say this when I would reach out for help. Whether it was helping me to get brakes put on the car, trying to get lights on in my apartment, or any other necessity. He would say "Precious I'm married now." This would boil my insides. I felt as though the way I lived in my early twenties (and well before my twenties, after high school) were typical. I made mistakes. My dad never should have stopped parenting me. The time my dad brought a space heater to my apartment to keep the place warm, really hurt me. My heat had been shut off. I sent my son to stay with his grandmother and called and asked my dad for help. He came over with a small space heater and let me know this should work. Most times my dad would come up short, I just viewed it as him teaching me how to survive. I completely failed survival because here I was asking my dad if my son and I could move in. My son was *my* responsibility. *I* was supposed to protect him and love him. *I* promised him these things. Sorrow and embarrassment filled my soul. I began to question why I had bothered to go my dad for help. I was twenty-one years old, with a child, no college education, no direction, and possibly no place to live. Though my dad had said yes to letting my son and I move in, I knew he viewed me as a failure.

"Daddy, can we come to live with you? I am behind on my rent, the complex has changed management, and I am being put out." My dad turned and looked at me. His look pierced. He was mad.

"What!" My dad responded. I began to repeat what I had just asked, when he quickly cut me off and began to yell at me. He yelled that I did not listen. He was right I didn't. I did not listen. I was tired of just listening. It's like being in those classrooms, where the teacher provides direction for an assignment to be completed; yet doesn't take the time out to answer questions, nor provide examples. I had been hearing "Precious, I'm married now." for the longest; it was not helping me. It was only hurting me more and more. I was done listening to the response "No Precious." Anytime I would call my dad for any help; it was no. There was a time I caught the bus home from work. It was cold out and the bus took forever to come. My dad did not live far from where I was. I called him to pick me up. I also felt a bit unsafe. My dad explained why he could not pick me up that night. Now, I will say my dad would help sometimes. However, I heard no, more than I heard yes. I was tired of listening.

After yelling, and me shedding tears, my dad said we could come and live with him and his wife. God, I felt relieved. Though he had just busted my ear drums, my son would have a place to stay. My dad was there for us, in that moment. He could yell at me anytime. I just wanted a dad. I found gratitude in knowing I still had a parent who was here. I was not alone. After my mom passed, I felt as though I was in this big world alone. My dad was not around as much as he should have been. My opinion. So, to hear him say yes; warmed me. My dad told me to come with him upstairs to make his wife aware. We arrived in the kitchen, where my stepmother prepared lunch. My dad shared with my stepmom that I would be coming to live with them. My stepmother stopped preparing lunch, looked at me, and then my father. She responded,

"Oh no she is not! She will not move in here!"

Chapter 14

My stepmother and I did not have the best relationship. I felt she was the reason my dad stopped being a dad. I can also recall her saying some rude things to me, that I felt should not have been said to a nine or ten-year-old. There was a time when I was nine or ten and my dad had come by my mom's house to pick me up. My stepmother was with my father. My mom inquired if my father could help her with installing me and my brother's air conditioning unit. My dad agreed to help. As my stepmother and I waited in the car for my dad, my stepmother asked me why my mom's boyfriend couldn't install the units for my mom. Why was she asking me this? I was a kid. I didn't know. I didn't fully understand. Now that I am a woman, I understand. However, I disagree with pulling a child into grown folks' business.

Each time I would ask my dad for help with something he would always reference his marriage as to why he *couldn't* help. Isn't *two* supposed to better than *one?* When my mother passed away, I was only 19 years old. When my dad left the burial to head out of town, he left me. I cannot recall my dad calling to check on me and my son, who was just a baby. He did come to the house once to visit with my son, after he was born. I resented my stepmother for this. It's like I noticed the subliminal messages. So, when my stepmother said my son and I couldn't come and stay; it confirmed everything I had ever thought of her.

Tears filled my eyes as I stood in that kitchen. I became angry. My stepbrother was living there at that time, yet my son and I could not come to stay. This was how she worked. She would do things for her children, but it seemed she left me and my brother out to dry.

"Huh? My dad already said we could come to stay." I replied.

"I said you can't! This is my house!" My stepmother snapped back. She emphasized *"I"* and *"my."* It was like she always tried to prove a point that she was running the show. I did not care about her personal issues and personal ego. I just went to my dad because he was all I had left. This thought made me even more angry. She was trying to take away the only thing I had left. I yelled back at her in that moment.

"Your son stays here! Why can't I?!" I yelled. I couldn't help myself. I tried to hold back from yelling and being viewed as disrespectful. I knew this was wrong! Who was she to tell me I couldn't come to stay with my dad? Who did she think she was? She was not my mother. She did not care for me as her own. I always knew this. I couldn't understand why she felt so much resentment toward me. I didn't understand why she wanted to control everything! My stepmother looked at my dad, ignoring me and said,

"She can go to a shelter, her mouth is too smart, and I don't let disrespectful kids live with me!"

A shelter? I thought to myself. I knew in that moment I was going to lose it. I was going to snap, maybe use a little profanity, roll my eyes, become physical. She had just told my son and I to go to a shelter!

"A shelter!? I'm not going to a shelter!" I yelled back.

For some reason I could not say what I really wanted to say to her. I was so upset yet couldn't express it how I wanted to. My stepmother walked up to me and continued to yell at me. She said things along the lines of me having a house full of furniture and there was nowhere for my furniture to go. She even explained how one of her sisters, husband, and children went to a shelter once before. She explained that shelters could help me find a home. I just stood there and let her yell and say crazy things. Next thing you know I was leaving out of the house with my child and father, to head to a shelter.

The car ride was long and quiet. I stared out the window at the beautiful homes we drove pass. I wished for a new life. I felt numb to what had just taken place. I didn't say anything to my father. I knew if my mother was still on Earth none of this would have happened. My stepmother would not have suggested a shelter. She did this knowing I didn't have anyone. How pitiful. We pulled up in front of some building and my dad began to explain how I would need to come here to get assistance to find a home. Everything around me began to sound like I was under water. I didn't have a relationship with God at that time. I had no idea what was next. Yet, he was with me the entire time. He was with me in that very moment as I looked out the window and wondered how a father could send his daughter to a shelter. A tear fell down my face. I had no idea what my next move would be. God knew.

Chapter 15

So do not fear, for I am with you; do not be dismayed, for I am your God. I will strengthen you and help you; I will uphold you with my righteous right hand.

Isaiah 41:10 NIV

After leaving my dad's house that day, I knew I would never speak to him again. I had been chasing my father for years, and always wondered why I had to chase him. He had finally rejected me to my face. Through my anger I still felt sorry for him. How could he sleep at night knowing he transported his one and only daughter to a shelter? God has blessed my father tremendously. How could he not want his children to be a part of those blessings? I never really expressed what was in the box on the shelf with my father. I never asked about phone calls that went unanswered. Or why there was always an excuse. I decided to keep it in the box on the shelf. I felt as though my dad chose his wife over me. He just left me in this big world, that constantly spun. I was dizzy. I couldn't fight the things I was up against. He left me to fight alone. I thought I would never be able to forgive him.

I was able to keep my apartment. I guess that was the good out of that situation. I managed to hustle to assure that my son and I had a roof over our heads. We were not going to go to a shelter. I worked extra hours to catch up on rent payments. I also changed my budget. I sacrificed way more. No more shopping, nails, nor hair salons. I had business to take care of. God was on my side. During these times, I was so thankful to have my son with me. He gave me peace. I would come home from work, get settled with my son, read to him, and share laughs. He depended on me. I hesitated as I wrote my story, not knowing how my son would act toward life being revealed to him. He was only months old when these events took place.

I finally developed a routine. I must say a productive routine. I was back in school. I would work, attend school, and care for my son when we arrived home. Sometimes my son would attend night classes with me. Thank God for that professor. Things were starting to look up a bit. The alcohol, clubs, and boys were no longer in the picture. Just me and my baby.

A year later my apartment management switched. My rent increased, and I was a month behind on rent. Here we go again. I was being evicted again. The rules changed under the new management. They were looking to evict everyone and start fresh with new tenants. If you gave them any reason to evict you, you were being evicted. Though I was only behind a month. I decided to pack my things and move in with my sister. I would live with my sister, save money over the summer and move into a new place. Moving in with my sister allowed a fresh start. It allowed me to save money. Old habits came back. I met someone, began dating, and moved into his place.

It was in this relationship I had an epiphany. I heard that voice again. *"There is more."* This time is was different. It is like my desire shifted for change. I wanted peace. I did not have anything stored inside of me. I did not have a sense of who I was. I had spent the last few years packing boxes and storing them on shelves without taking the time to open the box and search to see what was inside. Instead, I just let my issues sit. I didn't want to identify what was wrong. I didn't attempt to find out who I was. I was only concerned about others being around me. It was like I needed people to be around me, to reassure my identity. Well, those people do not and did not define me. The new relationship I was in was not going to define me. The new home was not going to define me. I was only repeating the same things with different people. I wanted more for my son. I was hardworking and determined. I just kept placing myself in toxic situations.

Bills were due. I was left to pay them. I gave up, I'd had enough. In my new relationship we argued and fought. I packed clothes for my son, and I left the apartment. I left behind furniture; I didn't care. I wanted out. I felt lost again. It's like I just could not get it together! The past three years had been devastating. I went back to my dad's house. I had no choice.

Chapter 16

"When he came to his senses, he said, 'How many of my father's hired servants have food to spare, and here I am starving to death! I will set out and go back to my father and say to him: Father, I have sinned against heaven and against you." Luke 15:17-19 NIV

My stepmother opened the door to see me standing there with tears running down my face. I stood in humility. I needed help. I was giving up on life. The thought of taking my own life, haunted me! I knew I needed to get help. I had to live for my son. My life had been so fast over just a few years. I just couldn't catch a break. So many things kept trying to attach to my life. I just wanted a fresh start. I wonder, did I ever really have a start? My life took off when my mother passed. I didn't take time for anything but the fast train. I would have this repetitive dream of me driving a car and my vision would become blurry. I would become filled with fear and anxiety of the thought of crashing. I never crashed. This was a representation of my life. I wasn't seeing clearly. I was on my journey headed to destiny. Yet my vision was not clear. No clear vision and no direction. I needed direction. I lost my mother at 19 years old. I had just graduated high school and had not learned how to navigate through life. It was time for me to get those teachings. My mother had done her best. As I

mentioned before, she taught me how to balance a check book, open a

savings and checking account and many other things, at the age of fifteen. I

needed to revisit those lessons. I needed an instructor. A parent.

I looked at my stepmother with tears rolling down my face.

"I am sorry. Please help me I can't do this anymore. I don't want to live, I

have nowhere to go, my son needs me, please help!" She grabbed me

before I could finish and hugged me. She began to cry as well. She said,

"yes" with urgency in her tone. She continued to repeat yes, as we hugged.

She took my hand and walked me up the stairs to my father who rested in

their bedroom. She explained to my dad that I would be moving in with my

son, and that they had to help me get on my feet. Just like that, the deal was

sealed. It's like they both waited for me to return.

My stepmother later shared with me, while starting to build our

relationship; that my father attended a church service with her one day and

began to cry. She explained, that as he cried, he referred to his daughter

being out in the world all by herself. She said from that moment forward

they made a vow that if any of their children came seeking shelter, or any

assistance they would commit to helping. God was working and in control

the entire time. My dad was right. I was in a huge world all alone. There was

so much I had gone through. I was so happy to finally be under some

parental guidance.

Shortly after the birth of my son I played in this real world. Meeting people, hanging out, drinking, smoking, at one time I even attempted ecstasy. My mother always warned me about drugs. There I was living a life of darkness and disobedience. I was lost. I would drink with friends and drive drunk. Not caring about consequences, or even thinking there could be consequences. I behaved as if I did not have two excellent parents that raised me. I believe God flashed a vision before my father's eyes of what was going on with me.

Chapter 17

While staying with my father and stepmother I found so much peace. I went back to school and continued to work full time. My son was still on my side every step of the way. My focus was always my son. Minus the wildlife. My dad and stepmother agreed that I would continue to pay rent to remain responsible. I agreed as well. I didn't want to fall into not paying bills. I didn't want to become comfortable. We agreed I would live there for six months and then begin to search for my own apartment. During that time, my stepmother and I began to talk more. She shared with me, that I was nothing like what she'd thought. She was right. I wasn't. Though I never meant ill will, or had any bad intentions, I'm sure my pain showed. She and I would talk about life. She was a teacher. She would talk to me about savings, building credit, and so much more. I was, and still am truly grateful for her.

As we go through life, we all must understand each of us have our own journey. Our God is speaking to us all, correcting us all, and preparing us all. My stepmother may have had a conversation with God as well. She also may have been going through her own pain. Who knows, we are pass that. I was able to forgive both my father and stepmother. One night, while living with them, I came home and handed my stepmother the money for

staying there. She looked so surprised. I was a day early. She commended me

on how responsible I was and allowed me to hang out that night and offered

to babysit my son. I felt so good. I was being responsible and earning my free

time. Work hard, play hard. Before, I was always responsible and paid bills

on time. However, distractions, stress and depression got the best of me. At

my dad's home there were no distractions. Something was different. I had

support. Most important, I had love. I was motivated to do the right thing.

It felt good to handle business. I will say this, to all my readers, we should

not solely depend on the support of others to accomplish what we need. The

power is in us. Despite the circumstances around us.

As I write, I realize I was also happy to be with my father. I was

happy to be under shelter. Under his shelter. My mother was gone. I was a

young parent. I felt safe being at my dad's house. I knew being there I was

protected. That was all I had ever wanted. I was getting back to myself. My

mental state was calm. It was a sense of relief for my stepmother to finally

see who I really was and vice versa. I never wanted her to view me as someone

who was disrespectful. My mother and I had a great relationship. Of course,

my mom would have to discipline me at times; however, our love for one

another was greater. I could only imagine where we would be today. I was a

young woman who cared about life. I was a hard worker and determined. I

had goals and wanted to accomplish them. When I decided to suppress my feelings of everything that had hurt me, I didn't do myself a favor. This only made things worse. I never thought it could have gotten that worse, but hey, it could have been worse. When my mother passed away, I knew life had to go on, so I decided to go through life fast. That way, I wouldn't have to deal with the fact that I no longer had my mother. That my son would never meet his grandmother. Feelings of being alone. Screaming for help but no one listened. I thought if I zoom through life, I would not have time to remember reality. I was wrong.

While staying with my dad, I attended school and became a licensed Esthetician. Finishing school made me proud. I was doing what I loved to do. I began to build up clientele with waxing services. Life was going so well. My son was growing each day. I was a busy mother, yet always made time for my little one. He was my biggest motivation. I would attend class during the day and work during the evenings. My son's grandmother would assist with keeping my son while I worked. Life had completely turned around for me. I was no longer hanging out in clubs, chasing boys, drinking alcohol. I was a mother first and a student.

Chapter 18

"Ask, and it shall be given you; seek and ye shall find; knock, and it shall be opened unto you." Matthew 7:7 KJV

I moved out of my dad's home and moved into my own apartment. This was a great accomplishment. I managed to meet my goal in six months! My son had his own bedroom and backyard to play in. I was so thankful to God that we had managed to get a fresh start. My stepmother was extremely proud of me and assisted me with finding a place to live. Our relationship did a complete 180. We became so close. We would talk often, and she would provide advice anytime I needed it. I was thankful for her. See understand, things do not always start off smooth. All things must grow. She and I both grew as individuals. I spent a lot of time reflecting and thinking once I moved into my own place. I guess I was finally allowing myself to go into those boxes on the shelves. When attempting to reach for a box, I would stop. I would shift my thinking to something else. Making sure to stay on the surface. Not wanting to go any deeper. Again, this was not good for me.

Each day I would find myself forcing myself away from my past. See, the thing is, when you're dealing with hurt, in order to heal, you must truly understand the root of your hurt. Many times, people go through life hurting, not understanding why nor attempting to begin to understand. I needed to understand why. I continued to think I could figure this out on my own. It would only get worse. I would find myself in a deep depression. Not understanding why. I would always wish my mother were present so I could cry in her arms. Maybe talk things through. Life had moved along, and I had not fully understood nor grasped what had taken place. I will say I was incredibly grateful to have overcome so much in such little time. However, there was something missing. Therefore, I deeply believe our purpose here on Earth is far greater than anything else. We are children of God who have all been born with a purpose. As we walk through life our purpose is revealed to us. It is not an overnight thing. It does not just happen at the snap of a finger. Sanctification is a process. My dad once shared with me that without God there is no peace. I held on to his words. I had experienced suicidal thoughts again, and my dad shared this with me at that time. As we sat on my front steps at my home, I continued to share with my dad how confused I was. I had my son, money, accolades, but I didn't feel truly happy. My dad said, "You know Precious, without God; we don't have peace."

I had tried everything else in life. Nothing worked. That's exactly what it was! I had been successful in areas of my life; however, I didn't have peace. I did not have God's peace. I didn't have a relationship with God. I may have experienced happy days, however, I desired peace. I immediately began looking for a bible my mother had given to me and my siblings before she passed away. The memory came back to me of my mother and I sitting on my Aunt's couch. As we watched the music video by Alicia Keys "Nonone" my mother said, *"She is singing to the Lord."* I thought back to the time I had fallen off my bicycle. I was in extreme pain and could only call on Jesus. I recalled the day I was in church and was filled with the Holy Spirit. All these memories filled not only my mind but my heart as I sought out the Lord. I pulled the bible from a box, sat down and began to read.

Chapter 19

Come unto me, all ye that labour and are heavy laden, and I will give you rest.

Matthew 11:28.

As I read God's word. I believed. What I'd felt had been missing was there all along. My God was there. I decided to attend church service, to allow myself to go deeper into the understanding of God's word. I also began to fellowship. My son would join me. I became committed to reading God's word day and night ensuring to teach my son the word of God. My son and I would pray together. I dedicated my life to the Lord on Mother's Day. Afterward, my son and I were baptized.

But seek ye first the kingdom of God, and his righteousness; and all these things shall be added unto you. Matthew 6:33 KJV

I began to seek God in all that I did. My life became a life of worship. It again, revealed, that God was with me the entire time. Not only was he with me, he was with my son. The Lord gave me my son. When I became pregnant my mother said everything would be okay. It was! Everything was OK! God's grace is sufficient! As a young parent, God provided strength for me to be able to care for my son. Not only did I care for my son, my God supplied the resources, the finances, and the people to support. Not only did God provide, he walked with me. His word promised that he would never leave me nor forsake me. During the days of struggle, fornication, partying, alcohol abuse, grief, molestation, God was with me all along.

I immediately knew I did not want to go back to my old life I'd lived before. That peace, my dad spoke of, was finally present in my life. I began to meditate on the scripture *Galatians 5:22*. The fruit of the Spirit. I was aware of my approach to people, my attitude, and my posture. I wanted to love on people. I found it in my heart to forgive my father. I knew that my father had his own journey. I began to understand how even during those trials with my father, I was able to continue to love him, not because of me, but because of Christ. The Lord has made us all in his image. We must not be ashamed of this.

I forgave my father in my heart. I wanted my father to be blessed. Did I still desire a relationship with my father? Of course. He's my father. However, I no longer needed to hold on to things of the past. The Lord was literally doing a new thing in my life. That meant those connected to me during that time as well. I decided to cling to the new thing. Did this mean that all would be perfect? No way! Life could and would still happen. I just knew **whose** I was. I knew how to get through this life. God's word lead me to self-reflect. Look inward. It allowed me to stop looking at everyone and how they affected me. I began to look at myself, and how I treated others. I began to live to please God. In pleasing God, we please one another. My faith led me to believe that God's word is active; always moving. The fruit of the spirit was being nurtured daily by God's word. I became obedient to God's word. Was I perfect? Maybe at the very beginning of becoming saved. Just kidding! None of us are perfect. Even if our desire is to be perfect. It is just not possible in this flesh. We must die to the flesh daily. Daily I worked on killing my flesh. I did this through prayer, studying God's word, fellowshipping, and fasting. (I continue to do this even today- this never stops. Sanctification is a process.) If my physical body was not acting in sin; I am sure my mind was. Therefore, I say, we are not perfect. This is okay. However, we should always be striving to make our Lord and Savior smile. That's what it was. My desire was to please God and not man. I no longer cared what man thought of me. I no longer needed to fit in with everything that was going on around me. I changed. My outer and inner appearance changed. The inner was most important. It started with my mind. My heart was then softened.

Chapter 20

I decided to practice abstinence. The Lord began to show me my past. It was revealed to me that I was molested as a young child. I was also molested at the age of thirteen. The year I lost my virginity. I would always hear stories about women who were promiscuous, were usually fatherless, and had been molested. The "Daddy Issue Are Real and Can Affect Your Sex Life, Study Says" (2020) website explains that researchers found that fathers who were divorced had a greater influence on their daughter's sexual behavior. The article explained that daughters who had their fathers in the home as they grew; were less likely to engage in sexual behavior, use of drugs, and alcohol. The opposite would take place with the daughter who did not have a father in the home. The article then says, "daddy issues does exist." It was revealed to me that I had *daddy issues*. With those daddy issues, many other issues came along. I never wanted to affiliate myself with the findings from the article above. I didn't want to think the relationship with my father may have led me to act in certain ways. It did. I had to identify that and accept it. I had to call it for what it was.

I decided to practice abstinence. I needed to cleanse myself from this act.

I never wanted to give myself to another man if he was not my husband. I prayed to the Lord and asked the Lord to help me with this. I asked the Lord to give me strength. I was abstinent for a little over a year. During that time, I was able to develop an intimate relationship with the Lord. I was amazed at God's work. Fornication no longer had power over me. I was no longer in bondage. I had forgiven my father and died to fornication. I no longer held on to these things. See how it's a domino effect? I was angry with my father, that anger grew into resentment. That resentment grew into an act. A cry out. SEX! I traded those in, for the things the Lord promised. MY JOY! Joy is the settle assurance that everything will be okay. I have many well rested nights now!

I decided to go back to school. I also began doing small jobs under my Esthetician License. I walked in purpose. I no longer entertained things that were not sent by God. During this time, I would have dreams where a demonic being would attempt to attack me in my sleep, sexually. There were times when I awakened, I would find scratches on my body. I would call on the name of Jesus when this would happen. I learned that I would be taunted by demonic beings, to attempt to make me fall into old behaviors. I began to pray and fast. During fasting and prayer, the Lord revealed that he would provide my son and I a home. He revealed to me a vision of a front lawn with green grass. There was plenty of yard in the vision. The Lord revealed this during praise and worship as well. I praised the Lord and thanked Him!

I began to prepare to purchase a home. I began to save money. I was a full-time waitress at the time. I began to save tips. I realized I was not spending much time with my son at the time and wanted to change that. I began to pray and ask the Lord to provide a job which would allow me to spend more time with my son. I continued to wait tables and provide waxing services. I continued to save, pay off debt, and pray. I meditated on *Isaiah 43:18-19kjv*. I did not focus on things of old; I focused on the new thing that God was doing in my life. It was nothing that I was doing. It was God alone. My role was to praise, and practice obedience.

Suddenly the process began of me purchasing my first home. I was excited and most important grateful. I was a single mother who was purchasing her first home at the age of twenty-six. The Lord provided the right people, the finances, as well as patience. The process was long. There was a lot of back and forth. I was responsible for paying off things before moving forward. I managed to provide all items which were being requested to get approved for a home loan.

Chapter 21

As I sat at the closing table, the scripture from Matthew 6:25-26 KJV came to my heart. *Therefore, I say unto you, take no thought for your life, what ye shall eat, or what ye shall drink; nor yet for your body, what ye shall put on. Is not the life more than meat, and body than raiment? Behold the fowls of the air: for they sow not, neither do they reap, nor gather into barns; yet your heavenly Father feedeth them. Are ye not much better than they?* I smiled. The Lord was providing the entire time. He knew this day would come years before the day. The nights I would cry. The nights I danced all night in the club. The nights I consumed too much alcohol. The day I rode to that shelter and looked out the window at those beautiful homes. He knew this day would come. This day had already taken place. I just had not walk into it yet.

The scripture also revealed to me that there is more to life. This goes back to my feeling as a child. The desire, is what was attempting to lead me. The Holy Spirit. There is so much more to life than material things. God's peace is victory! Yes, I was super excited for becoming a first-time home buyer. Yet, I understood there is more. The *house* would not *make* me. So many times in the world we become wrapped up in material things. Our accolades are what makes us. Our bank account, our status in this world. I desired to remain humble. I desired to not worship my home, nor the accomplishment. For, it was the Lord's doing.

Many people feel that we do these things on our own. I must go off my experience. When I had nowhere to go, no shelter, not only did the Lord allow me to keep my apartment during that season. He provided even more. My own home. Do you see how this was not my doing? Have you ever been in a situation where you try to plea with the Lord? *"God, if you just get me out of this one, I will worship you always."* You say this with faith, you say this knowing *you* are not worthy. Let me tell you, you do not have to go to church every day to say a statement as such to the Lord. I recall times calling upon the Lord before studying his word or attending a church. There are times when we feel as though we have hit rock bottom. We may not know which way to turn. However, we know to call upon the Lord. Therefore, in our request, when he answers our prayers, why do most feel it was their doing, afterward? Their accomplishment. I always think just as easy as it comes it can be taken away. I see it as my Father in Heaven supplied a home for my son and I. Thank you Father.

Chapter 22

As my son and I stood outside of our new home we both smiled. We took pictures holding the "SOLD" sign. We were both happy. We were ready for our new journey. The Lord had brought us such a long way. I continued to raise my son and press toward completing school.

It is amazing what the Lord can do for us when we just allow Him. I always felt as though I was running from something. Most say we run from the calling on our lives. I believe this is true. In my case, I ran from love as well. I spent so many years chasing everything else, which was in the opposite direction of the authentic love. I continued to get further and further away from it. The beauty of it all, is that the Lord continued to walk with me. The day I turned and faced Him was the day my life changed. As stated before, this does not make me exempt from life. However, his grace and mercy cover me all my days. As children of God we do not use tools of this world to get through life. We live a life of worship. We live a life to please God.

If you find yourself in a situation that is not the best, know that you're standing in God's promises. God does not begin to love and care for you the moment you accept Him into your life. When you're out in the world, He's with you. I wanted to share my story with my readers so my readers could see that God is with us all our life. Even before the womb. *"Before I formed thee in the belly, I knew thee; and before thou camest forth out of the womb I sanctified thee, and I ordained thee a prophet unto the nations." Jeremiah 1:5 KJV*

God is with us before we are formed. Our lives are set out by God before we are formed. Do you know the amazing revelation in this scripture? God KNEW us! We connected on an intimate level with our Father before Earth. Therefore, when He calls us, we recognize His voice. Therefore, when sin is present, we feel like something is off. We know the right thing to do. Yet we may struggle. He is the Most High God! He is our creator. He knows us. We must trust Him! Your relationship with God is intimate. It is nothing to be ashamed of. I would have some people say to me; "You're on your God thing again." These people would criticize me during my struggle of walking with God. The enemy will always attempt to make you feel as though you are a failure. Remember the devil says the opposite of what God says. You must remember you are not perfect. God calls us to repent. We must repent daily. When we think we have done it all right. When we think we have no sin in us. When we think we have made it to the finish line. We must seek God. Ask him to show us our hearts. In the bible there is a parable of the man who explained he had done all things right. He was instructed to sale all his possessions. The man was not able to do so. The parable showed how we may think we measure up to God himself; however, there will always be something we lack. For if we had it all, could do it all, we would not need a Savior.

During your walk with God, once you have fully surrendered, you will lose certain relationships. Everyone will not understand your journey nor your desire. You must continue the walk. When those people would claim I was doing my "God thing", I knew they did not understand the word of God. They were so use to their traditions that they were numb to the movement of God's word. In my challenges during my walk, those people would have prayed for me. Those people would have talked through things with me. They would have come for that lost sheep.

There will be trial and errors. Surround yourself around those who will pray you through. Pray and ask God to bless you with sisters and brothers in Christ who will pray you through and be a listening ear when need. We must learn to apply the word of God in all areas of our lives. We cannot do this alone. God has called us to fellowship. God has called us to pray together.

There were also times when people would envy my desire and walk to please God. The scripture says *"There hath no temptation taken you but such as is common to man: but God is faithful, who will not suffer you to be tempted above that ye are able; but will with the temptation also make a way to escape, that ye may be able to bear it." 1 Corinthians 10:13 KJV.* The scripture explains that temptation is common to all men. All people. Temptation will take place. Yet God is FAITHFUL- HE WILL PROVIDE A WAY TO ESCAPE. That way to escape is a desire to do right, and strength to walk in obedience. If you are wanting to practice abstinence because you are not married. DO IT! Do not let *"people"* tell you it is impossible. Instead praise God that he has provided a way of escape. The desire to do right. Follow him. There will be many times where others will judge, however, you must continue to focus on the prize. Salvation.

Chapter 23

You may have noticed during my story, there were many cycles. Many of the same issues, same feelings, same outcomes. Those cycles today no longer exist. Once I surrendered my life, those cycles ended. During the times before surrendering my life, my life was filthy. It was dark. It was toxic. Don't get me wrong, it took me to come to the other side to realize how filthy my life was. Before while in it, I could not tell. Let me tell it, I was living my best life. Yea right!

I began to journal. Journaling helped me to study scripture and write out how I could and would apply scripture to my life. Journaling also allowed me to express my thoughts on paper. This was something I always did as a kid. I got away from it in my adult life. Things that you loved to do when you were a kid, do them! I am sure whatever it was you loved doing as a kid, may just be your passion. I would journal about reaching goals. I would journal about conflict resolution. I would journal about God's peace. I just wrote. Writing was a relief, and still is a way release for me. Some people like to exercise, some like to listen to music. Some go for a walk. I like to write.

God reveals our purpose to us during an intimate relationship with Him. Spending quality time with God is more than just going to church on Sunday. Do not let someone fool you. Having a relationship with God is more than just being the lead singer in the choir. How about stop everything you're doing. Now, tune into God. Meditate on His word. Study it. Pray for understanding. God is always speaking. He is always moving. Most important; listen.

As I began to study the scriptures, I realized in all my circumstances, I was standing in the promises of God. Every promise in the bible; we are standing in.

1. "The Lord will fight for you; you need only to be still" Exodus 14:14

2. "If my people, who are called by my name, will humble themselves and pray and seek my face and turn from their wicked ways, then I will hear from heaven, and I will forgive their sin and will heal their land." 2Chronicles 7:14

3. "For I know the plans I have for you, declares the Lord, plans to prosper you and not to harm you, plans to give you hope and a future." Jeremiah 29:11

4. "So if the Son sets you free, you will be free indeed." John 8:36

5. "Therefore I tell you, whatever you ask for in prayer, believe that you have received it, and it will be yours." Mark 11:24

6. "Have I not commanded you? Be strong and courageous. Do not be afraid; do not be discouraged, for the Lord your God will be with you wherever you go." Joshua 1:9

7. "Even though I walk through the darkest valley, I will fear no evil for you are with me; your rod and your staff, they comfort me." Psalm 23:4

8. "The Lord is a refuge for the oppressed, a stronghold in times of trouble. Those who know your name trust in you, for you, Lord, have never forsaken those who seek you." Psalm 9:9-10

9. "Do not be anxious about anything, but in every situation, by prayer and petition, with thanksgiving, present your requests to God. And the peace of God, which transcends all understanding, will guard your hearts and your minds in Christ Jesus." Philippians 4:6-7

10. "If you declare with your mouth, Jesus is Lord, and believe in your heart that God raised him from the dead, you will be saved. For it is with your heart that you believe and are justified, and it is with your mouth that you profess your faith and are saved." Romans 10:9-10

Those are only a few of God's promises. It is said there are over 5,000 promises which can be found in the Holy Bible. Let's get to it. Let's learn about our Father, and what he has promised. Let's learn what our role is. How do we live a life to please God? He has provided us with instruction. He has also provided the Holy Spirit. When you're in a place and you feel that intuition saying, "maybe it's time to leave." Listen. The Holy Spirit is speaking. Obedience is better than sacrifice. Get in tune with what the Lord is saying. He is always speaking.

Chapter 24

I decided to tell my story in hopes to encourage readers. We have all gone through something in this lifetime. Have we all tried God? I did not grow up in the church as a little girl. I didn't fall into tradition. Believe it or not, I would have never imagined myself in the position I am in today. If you're feeling like there is more to your life…. there is. If you're feeling like your trying to *"fit"* in…. you are. If you're feeling alone…. you're not. You too, are standing in God's promises. Life must happen; it has its ups and downs. We are not exempt from this. I could have committed suicide. If I would have done that, I wouldn't be here to raise my son. How would that have affected him? How would that have affected my family? I could have stayed angry with my father forever. How would that have affected me? To carry anger is equivalent to carrying bricks. Who wants to haul around bricks everyday all day? Release that to the Lord. Forgive people and stop holding grudges. Everyone has their own journey. Everyone has their own conversation with the Lord. The Lord loves us all and knows each and everyone of us. Let go of old things that are dead and have no life. Those things are no longer effective in your life. It's like a flower that has wilted away. It does not serve any purpose. It's like wine being in old wineskins.

Remember, everything must grow. Our God is a God of growth. Leave the dead to the dead.

When you accept the new things coming your way, those connected to you will receive as well. That's the beauty of forgiveness also. We can be free. Know who you are. Will you know who you are completely? Maybe not, because we are growing as individuals daily. Our God knows. Inquire with the Lord the will for your life. Be still long enough to hear from God. Go into those boxes on the shelves and pull everything out. Examine what the hurt is, and where it stems. My hurt was resenting my father, I turned to boys, who would provide affection. After affection I was okay for a little bit, then I would hurt again, and repeat the steps. A cycle. How do we break that cycle? We can't do it alone. We must allow our heavenly Father in. Once you do this, you will see time as never before. Time should not be wasted. Time is precious. Your life has just begun! Your standing in the promises of God. Go get what is yours!

The Desire

"Come, follow me," Jesus said, "and I will send you out to fish for people."

The desire of writing my story and sharing it with those who know

me personally as well as those who do not; is for my readers to be

encouraged even in the low moments of their life. When you are going

through, please know you are not alone. A day will come which will set

you free. So many times, people believe that when they live in sin God

wants nothing to do with them. God wants nothing to do with sin. He

wants everything to do with you. Nothing can separate us from our

Father in Heaven. I did not grow up in church. Yet God still met with

me and talked with me. I hear so many people say, church is not a place

for people like me. Try not to focus on church, or what people will

think of you. Know what God thinks of you. So many times, when God is spoken of, people automatically measure with church. I encourage

you to pick up the bible. Church is great- however that shall pass. God's

word will not. Pick up the bible and begin to read. As a child I began to

read the word of God before stepping foot into a church. When I did

step foot in that church God called my name and I recognized his voice.

I will continue to pray for you and with you through your journey. May

God Bless you.

Precious C.

REFLECT

1. Do you have a sense of purpose? Are you walking in purpose? What is your purpose? What does purpose mean to you? Philippians 2:12-13

2. What are your interest and hobbies? John1:8

3. What is a promise God has promised you?

4. What are you doing to please God? Romans 12:1-2

Self Reflect

_____

_____

_____

_____

_____

_____

_____

_____

_____

_____

_____

_____

_____

_____

_____

_____

_____

_____

_____

_____

_____

_____

_____

_____

Made in the USA
Columbia, SC
08 June 2020